Cambridge **Discovery Education**™

▶ **INTERACTIVE READERS**

Series editor: Bob Hastings

LIFE ON THE EDGE
EXTREME HOMES

B1

Brian Sargent

CAMBRIDGE
UNIVERSITY PRESS

Discovery
EDUCATION™

CAMBRIDGE UNIVERSITY PRESS
Cambridge, New York, Melbourne, Madrid, Cape Town,
Singapore, São Paulo, Delhi, Mexico City

Cambridge University Press
32 Avenue of the Americas, New York, NY 10013-2473, USA

www.cambridge.org
Information on this title: www.cambridge.org/9781107630284

First published 2014

Printed in Hong Kong, China, by Golden Cup Printing Company Limited

A catalog record for this publication is available from the British Library.

Library of Congress Cataloging-in-Publication Data

Sargent, Brian, 1969-
 Life on the edge : extreme homes / Brian Sargent.
    pages cm. -- (Cambridge discovery interactive readers)
 ISBN 978-1-107-63028-4 (pbk. : alk. paper)
 1. Dwellings--Juvenile literature. 2. English language--Textbooks for foreign speakers.
 3. Readers (Elementary) I. Title.

GT172.S37 2013
392.3'6--dc23

                              2013023918

ISBN 978-1-107-63028-4

Additional resources for this publication at www.cambridge.org

Layout services, art direction, book design, and photo research: Q2ABillSMITH GROUP
Editorial services: Hyphen S.A.
Audio production: CityVox, New York
Video production: Q2ABillSMITH GROUP

Contents

Before You Read:
Get Ready!

Both people and animals in different parts of the world live in some surprising homes. Some are just unusual, but others are dangerous as well.

Words to Know

Look at the photos and read the sentences below. Then label the photos with the correct highlighted words.

_____ _____ _____ _____

1 Many ants live in an ant colony.

2 When people find something like gold, they make a discovery.

3 A ghost town is a town where no one lives.

4 A tent is a shelter used when camping.

? APPLY

People and animals sometimes choose very strange places to live. Where is the strangest place you have ever visited?

Words to Know

Read the paragraphs. Use the highlighted words to complete the sentences below.

The world can be a dangerous place. In places near the ocean, there are sometimes tsunamis, giant waves that can cover the land with water. When there is a tsunami, people need to protect themselves by getting to higher land.

Other places have volcanoes. When volcanoes erupt, they send clouds of hot ash high into the sky. People who live nearby, the local residents, must run for shelter.

Extreme weather is also dangerous. Sometimes it rains too much and there are floods. Other times it doesn't rain at all and there are droughts.

1 Floods are a kind of _____ weather.

2 Smoke sometimes comes from the top of _____.

3 Many beach areas have alarms to warn people about _____.

4 People who live in an area are called _____.

5 Some old volcanoes are safe. They are unlikely to _____.

6 After something has burned, there is _____.

7 It was a terrible _____; it didn't rain for a year.

8 _____ yourself from bad weather with a good tent.

CHAPTER 1

Unlikely Homes

**SEE WHAT LIFE IS LIKE IN THESE
UNLIKELY HOMES.**

Describe your perfect home. Would it be comfortable, with lots of space? Would you like a yard or maybe a garden? Maybe you would like theaters or a library nearby.

Or would you like something more **extreme**? If so, why not move to Scott Base? Scott Base has thirty bedrooms, modern bathrooms, and its own professional cook! There's a room with comfortable chairs for relaxing, reading books, or watching videos. If you prefer to be outside, Scott Base has a lot to offer, too. There is a field for skiing, and even a golf course for the summer months.

There is one small problem: Scott Base is in Antarctica. If you want to play golf there, you should bring a jacket, or two, or three. Summer temperatures at Scott Base almost never climb above 0°C. The golf balls they use are pink, so they can be found easily in the ice and snow.

Scott Base is a **research** center for scientists studying things like Antarctica, wildlife, and climate change. There are many research bases in Antarctica. Some, like Belgium's modern Princess Elisabeth Station, are only open during Antarctica's summer months, November to February. Others, like New Zealand's Scott Base, are open all year.

In Antarctica, winter temperatures drop very low. Between the months of March and October, the average temperature for Scott Base is around −30°C. (That's cold, but it's not the coldest temperature ever measured on Earth. That was −89.2°C at Russia's Vostok Station in 1983.)

The cold isn't the only problem. Winter brings 24-hour darkness to Antarctica. For people staying through the winter at Scott Base, the last sunshine they see is in April. They don't see the sun again until late August. Of course, summers in the Antarctic have the opposite problem: 24-hour sunlight. Both extremes can make it difficult for the people who live there to work and sleep.

?

ANALYZE

Imagine you are moving to Antarctica for one year starting tomorrow. What should you take with you?

Many kinds of workers, including researchers, electricians, mechanics, and cooks, live at Scott Base. Most workers live there for either six or thirteen months. However, if you have special training and you enjoy the cold and dark, perhaps there's an even more extreme place for you to live. Why not try the International Space Station?

The International Space Station (ISS) is 350 kilometers above the Earth and traveling at 28,000 kilometers per hour. Because the ISS is traveling so fast, it takes two days to get there. A spaceship must match its speed before it can connect with the station.

There are always six people living at the ISS, though most visitors stay less than six months. Each person is given a closet-sized bedroom, but the bedrooms have no beds. Beds are useless in zero gravity.[1] Showers are useless, too. Most people in the station clean themselves with wet towels.

[1] **zero gravity:** Gravity makes things fall to the ground; in space there is no gravity.

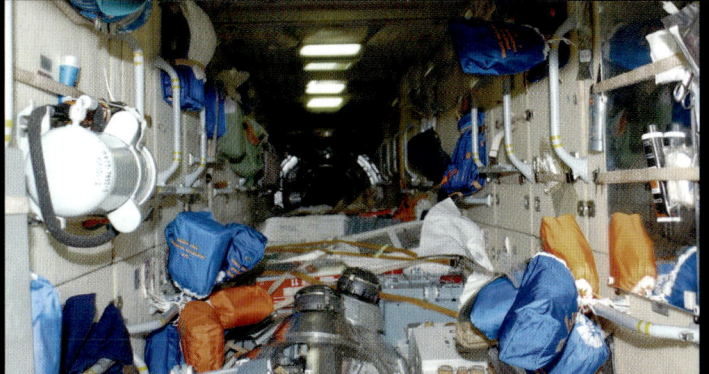

The ISS has an area for cooking and lots of food for its **residents**. However, eating can be a problem. On Earth, we use gravity to help us swallow food. In space, swallowing is more difficult. Many people say it is a lot like eating while lying down.

If you do plan on visiting the ISS, be prepared to be very busy. There are jobs to do almost every hour of the day, including two hours of exercising. People in zero gravity must work hard at staying fit. Otherwise, their return to Earth's gravity could be too hard on their body. Sometimes, when people return from the ISS, they must be carried away on stretchers[2] because they are too weak to walk.

....
[2]**stretcher:** something flat used to carry someone who is ill or cannot walk

CHAPTER 2

Dangerous Homes

WOULD YOU LIVE AT A PLACE CALLED "FIRE MOUNTAIN"? THOUSANDS OF PEOPLE IN INDONESIA DO.

Scott Base and the ISS are **temporary** homes. People who choose to live in those extreme places know they will stay there for only a few months. But around the world there are **permanent** homes that are more extreme, and more dangerous. People have lived in many of these places for thousands of years. One such place is Indonesia's Mount Merapi, also known as "Fire Mountain."

Mount Merapi is in the center of the island of Java, one of the world's most densely³ populated islands. The 2,911-meter tall mountain is an active volcano, extremely active. It erupts regularly, every five to ten years, and that makes it a very dangerous home.

³**densely/dense: (adv/adj):** with a lot of people close together

A group of eruptions in October and November of 2010 covered the area in a cloud of hot ash. People driving cars 250 kilometers from the volcano had to turn on their lights because of the darkness caused

by the ash cloud. Near Mount Merapi, over 300 people were killed and over 100,000 had to get away fast. Most left with just the clothes they were wearing and had to live in tents or other temporary shelters.

Even with its history of eruptions, many people still choose to live near Mount Merapi. One reason is the dense population on Java – around 1,000 people for every square kilometer. With so little space, some people must live in places others feel are too dangerous. Another reason is farming. The rich land around Mount Merapi is perfect for farmers to grow many types of plants.

Video Quest

Kamchatka

This video is about a place in far–east Russia. Watch it to find out how Kamchatka was built.

The residents around Mount Merapi have long known the danger that comes from living so close to a volcano. In other places around the world, people are just beginning to learn how dangerous their homes may be. Right now, the people of the Maldives are facing a danger they may never have expected.

The Maldives are made up of 1,190 small islands southwest of India. The country has a population of about 325,000 who live mostly on 200 of the islands. It also has a problem: The Maldives may not exist for much longer. They are slowly being covered by the sea.

Ice melting[4] in the Arctic is causing the sea to rise[5] a few millimeters every year. That may not seem like a lot, but it is to the Maldivians. The islands of the Maldives are very flat. About 80 percent of the islands are less than one meter above sea level. Even a small rise in sea level will make the islands smaller.

[4] **melt:** change from ice to water
[5] **rise:** move up

In 1987, an unusually high tide[6] covered most of the capital city of Malé. In 2004, a tsunami covered most of the islands, killing 82 people and leaving at least 12,000 more without homes. Now, the islands are smaller. Houses that used to be far from the beach are being washed away by the sea.

Scientists expect sea levels around the world to continue to rise, which is bad news for the people of the Maldives. If their islands are going to be completely covered by water, where will they go? The Maldives government is thinking about different ideas, including moving all the residents to other countries such as India or Australia. They must look to the future while looking out for the rising water.

[6]**tide:** the regular rise and fall of the sea

CHAPTER 3

Forgotten Homes

WHAT STORIES DO HOMES TELL AFTER THE PEOPLE LEAVE?

Long ago, many people believed there was a great island called Atlantis. Some said it was near Greece and had an army that once controlled much of Europe and Africa. Others placed the island near America and said its residents were peaceful and had advanced technology. Whatever people believed, they all agreed about one thing: Long ago, the island of Atlantis sank to the bottom of the ocean.

Today, most people believe that the story of Atlantis is a myth.[7] However, there are many lost homes around the world that are very real. Some can be found deep below the ground in Turkey: The underground cities of Cappadocia.

....

[7] **myth:** an ancient story, often one that explains something that happened in history or the natural world

Cappadocia is a popular tourist area in central Turkey. Above the ground are amazing sights, such as houses and temples[8] that have been cut from huge rock cliffs.[9] Under the ground, the sights are even more amazing.

The underground city of Kaymakli, built around 2000 BCE, has eight levels and includes everything a city might need. There are bedrooms, kitchens, as well as places to keep food and drink. There is also a temple and even a stable for horses. It is thought that 3,000 to 4,000 people lived in this large underground city. No one lives in it now, although the people who live in the village above sometimes still use Kaymakli's tunnels to get from place to place.

Kaymakli is one of many underground cities in Cappadocia. No one is exactly sure why these cities were built. Most likely it was to keep residents safe during wars.

[8]**temple:** a building where people pray
[9]**cliff:** an area of high rocks that go straight up

On the other side of the world from Cappadocia are very different forgotten homes. You can find small, forgotten towns, called ghost towns, in many places in the western part of the United States. Bodie, California, is one such town.

As is true with many ghost towns, people moved to Bodie originally because of gold. In the late 1800s, gold was found in the area and in less than 20 years, the town grew from almost nothing to a population of 10,000. Another 20 years later, most of the gold was gone, and the population fell to less than a thousand. A few years after that, not even a hundred people lived in the town.

Bodie State Historic Park

Now no one lives in Bodie. Over a hundred buildings are still there, including a jail, a school, and a post office. In 1962, California turned the entire town into a State Park. About 200,000 people visit the park each year. That's 20 times the number who lived there in the 1800s!

Some American ghost towns still have a little life in them. Terlingua, Texas, was once a mining[10] town of 2,000 people. They mined mercury[11] instead of gold, but, just like in Bodie, when the mines ran out of metal, most of the people left.

In the 1960s, however, Terlingua got new life when its few residents began an annual cooking competition. Now the Terlingua Chili[12] Cook-Off brings in tens of thousands of people every November to see who can cook the best chili. The rest of the year, the town's population is only a few hundred.

[10]**mining:** digging something out of the ground such as gold or coal
[11]**mercury:** silver-colored metal found in thermometers
[12]**chili:** a spicy dish made from meat and beans

CHAPTER 4

Animal Homes

WOULD YOU LIVE IN A HOME THAT WANTED TO EAT YOU?

A green parakeet

People may choose strange and dangerous places to live, but if you want to see some of the world's most dangerous homes, you have to look at animals. In Chapter 2, we learned about people living near one of the world's most active volcanoes. Can you imagine living *inside* an active volcano? A group of green parakeets in Nicaragua does just that. The toxic[13] smoke coming out of the Masaya volcano does not seem to bother them at all.

A home inside a volcano might seem safe to an animal like the clownfish. These small, colorful fish live in the warmer waters of the Indian and Pacific oceans, and they make their homes inside sea anemones.

---

[13]**toxic:** able to make a plant or animal get sick or die

Anemones are very beautiful but extremely dangerous animals that live on the ocean floor. They look similar to flowers, but they're covered with tentacles.[14] The anemones use their tentacles to sting[15] fish who get too close, then they catch them and eat them.

Clownfish live in sea anemones.

Clownfish choose sea anemones for food and **protection**. Nothing would try to eat a clownfish when it's hidden inside an anemone. For food, clownfish clean the anemones, eating plants that grow on them and bits of fish left over from the anemone's meals.

Even though the clownfish help the sea anemones, they must be very careful. To protect themselves from the anemones' sting, clownfish cover their bodies with a thin protective coat. When a clownfish chooses a sea anemone for a home, it lightly touches the tentacles with every part of its body to get used to the stings. If the fish ever lost its coat, the sea anemone would have a new name for the clownfish: dinner!

[14]**tentacle:** a long, thin part of some sea animals
[15]**sting:** put something harmful onto skin

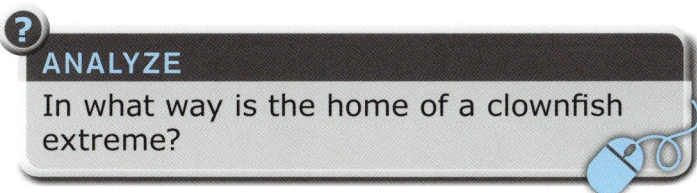

?

ANALYZE

In what way is the home of a clownfish extreme?

The leafcutter ant's home may not be as dangerous as the clownfish's, but it's still pretty extreme. Leafcutter ants are very, very small, but their homes are huge.

Leafcutter ants live in South America and some southern parts of North America. They are called leafcutter ants because they use their sharp jaws[16] to cut leaves from trees and plants. Then they bring the pieces home on their backs. Leafcutter ants are really hard workers. Some **colonies** can cut all the leaves off a small tree in just one day.

It's amazing to watch a line of leafcutter ants carrying bright green leaves, but it's even more amazing to see the home they bring them to. Leafcutter ants live in underground homes, covering as much as 50 square meters. In the colonies, special ants use the leaves to grow gardens of fungi[17] for food.

[16] **jaw:** the part of the mouth that contains teeth
[17] **fungi:** a type of plant like a mushroom

Leafcutter ant colonies are very organized. There are many rooms for gardening, but these underground gardens create a special problem. The gardens produce gases that could kill all the ants in the colony. To fix this, the ants build a system of vents[18] that bring in fresh air and take out the dangerous gases. In addition, the ants must build special tunnels that stop rain water from washing away the colony.

Recently, Dr. Bert Hölldobler wondered just how big leafcutter ant colonies truly are. To find out, he filled one with cement.[19] It took about 9,000 kilograms of cement to fill the colony, and when he dug out the dirt from around it, he saw that the colony went eight meters into the ground!

[18] **vent:** an opening that allows air, smoke, or gas to escape
[19] **cement:** gray powder that is mixed with water and sand to make a kind of stone
[20] **cattle ranch:** a large farm where cows are kept

Video Quest

Cattle Ranch[20]

Watch this video to see an unlikely home for cattle. How does the rancher's team get water for the cattle during a drought?

CHAPTER 5

Unlikely Life

LIFE CAN BE FOUND EVERYWHERE, FROM THE DEEPEST SEAS TO THE AIR HIGH ABOVE OUR HEADS.

In 1977, a team of scientists made an amazing discovery. The team, led by Dr. Robert Ballard, was looking for holes deep in the ocean called hydrothermal vents. Hydrothermal vents are small openings in the ocean floor. Super-hot water comes up through the holes and into the ocean.

The team was looking at the Galapagos Rift, an area of the Pacific Ocean about 2,500 meters deep. They were very pleased to find the hydrothermal vents, but they were also very surprised to find giant tubeworms living around the vents. People had thought it was impossible for animals to live so deep in the ocean. What were they getting food from? Where were they getting their energy from? The answer to both questions was the hydrothermal vents.

The water coming through the vents is very rich in chemicals like hydrogen sulfide. **Microorganisms**, near the vents take in the chemicals and change them to energy. Scientists had to make up a new word for the way animals produce energy from chemicals. They called it *chemosynthesis*.

Inside each tubeworm, there is a colony of these microorganisms. The tubeworms use the energy produced by the microorganisms as food.

Animals in the deep sea show that things can live in very unlikely places. Knowing this, scientists have looked for life in other unusual places. Recently, scientists in India found life in a place no one thought it could be: 40 kilometers above the Earth.

The scientists used a balloon to collect air from the stratosphere – an area high above our Earth. When they studied the air, they found microorganisms living there, including three new kinds, or species, never seen before. There are many questions about how the microorganisms got so high above the Earth, but one thing is certain: Life can make its home almost anywhere.

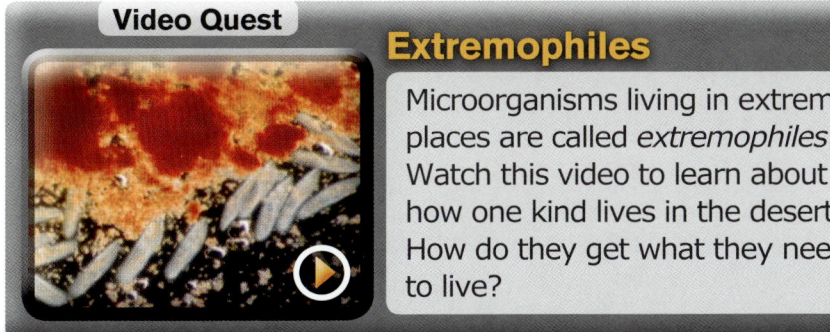

Video Quest

Extremophiles

Microorganisms living in extreme places are called *extremophiles*. Watch this video to learn about how one kind lives in the desert. How do they get what they need to live?

CHAPTER 6

What Do You Think?

READY TO MOVE TO AN EXTREME HOME? WHICH ONE WILL YOU CHOOSE?

In Chapter 1, you were introduced to life on a research base in Antarctica and on the International Space Station. Imagine you had to choose one of those places to live. Which would you choose? Would you prefer the long, dark winter of Antarctica or the small, closed space station?

There are no refrigerators in space. Fresh food must be eaten in just a few days after arriving at the ISS. However, during the long winter, some fresh fruit and vegetables can be grown at Antarctic bases in special indoor gardens.

Do you like salt and pepper? In space, you will have to use them in liquid form. Shaking salt over your food would send it everywhere! In Antarctica, you can shake salt and pepper all you want.

In Antarctica, there is no sunshine between April and August. However, at the ISS there is sunshine every 45 minutes. The ISS is traveling so fast, it goes completely around the world sixteen times in 24 hours!

Living in space may make you taller. When residents of Skylab, an early US space station, returned home, they had grown about three centimeters taller. Living in Antarctica will not change your height at all.

Inside both an Antarctic base and the ISS, you may dress normally. To go outside the base, however, you must wear many clothes to stay warm. To go outside the space station, you must wear a spacesuit!

In Antarctica, you sleep in a bed in a bedroom. In space, there are no beds. You sleep floating in a closet. Some people at the ISS were famous for sleeping anywhere when they got tired. They would close their eyes and float through the station until they woke up.

Much of the drinking water in Antarctica is made from seawater. Some of the drinking water at the ISS is made from the urine[21] of the residents.

What do you think? Where would you rather live?

[21] **urine:** the clear yellow liquid waste made by our bodies

After You Read

True or False?

Write T for True or F for False.

1 _____ Only scientists and researchers live in research stations in Antarctica.

2 _____ All life needs light to survive.

3 _____ It is possible to live near an active volcano.

4 _____ Microorganisms can live 40 kilometers above the Earth.

Multiple Choice

Choose the correct answer.

1 The underground cities of Cappadocia are in what country?
- Ⓐ United States
- Ⓑ Turkey
- Ⓒ Indonesia

2 Ghost towns were created when the people left. Why did they leave?
- Ⓐ Because they were afraid of ghosts
- Ⓑ Because they couldn't make money from the mines
- Ⓒ Because they wanted to move to America

3 How do microorganisms live at the bottom of the Galapagos Rift?
- Ⓐ They catch fish that swim down to the hydrothermal vents.
- Ⓑ They eat plants that grow on sea anemones.
- Ⓒ They make energy from chemicals coming from the hydrothermal vents.

4 Why are there no beds on the ISS?
- Ⓐ People don't need to sleep in space.
- Ⓑ In zero gravity, people can't lie down.
- Ⓒ People grow too tall for the beds.

Text Completion

Choose the correct word from the box to complete each sentence.

colony	myth	protect	temporary

1. Someday we may have a _____ on the moon.
2. My sister is living with us, but it is only _____.
3. Firemen _____ people from fire.
4. Some people believe Atlantis is real, but others call it
   a _____.

The Good and the Bad

Choose four of the unusual homes you read about. Then fill in the chart with the positive and negative things about each one.

Home	Positives	Negatives
1.		
2.		
3.		
4.		

Answer Key

Words to Know, page 4
1 colony **2** shelter **3** ghost town **4** discovery

Apply, page 4
Answers will vary.

Words to Know, page 5
1 extreme **2** volcanoes **3** tsunamis **4** residents
5 erupt **6** ash **7** drought **8** Protect

Analyze, page 7
Answers will vary.

Video Quest, page 11
Kamchatka was built by volcanoes.

Analyze, page 19
They live inside dangerous animals that could eat them.

Video Quest, page 21
They dig deep in the ground to find water for the cattle.

Video Quest, page 23
They live under stones in the desert that allow light to come through. They also get a little water.

True or False?, page 26
1 F **2** F **3** T **4** T

Multiple Choice, page 26
1 B **2** B **3** C **4** B

Text Completion, page 27
1 colony **2** temporary **3** protect **4** myth

The Good and the Bad, page 27
Answers will vary.